T0065683

STUDY GUIDE FOR
WHEN MY OX
GORES
MY NEIGHBOR

Using Hermeneutics to Travel
from Mt. Sinai to Mt. Zion

Josiah Nichols

WESTBOW
P R E S S®
A DIVISION OF THOMAS NELSON
& ZONDERVAN

WestBow Press books may be ordered through booksellers or by contacting:

WestBow Press
A Division of Thomas Nelson & Zondervan
1663 Liberty Drive
Bloomington, IN 47403
www.westbowpress.com
844-714-3454

Author credits: MDiv in biblical languages, BA in Bible and preaching ministry

ISBN: 978-1-6642-9251-2 (sc)
ISBN: 978-1-6642-9250-5 (e)

Library of Congress Control Number: 2023903064

Print information available on the last page.

WestBow Press rev. date: 02/22/2023

Contents

Chapter 1

Sinai Thunders

Secure sinners must bring the thundering of Mount Sinai before we bring them to Mt. Zion.

—George Whitefield[1]

Big Ideas

- Everyone has presuppositions and brings them to the text.
- Everyone has backgrounds that influence their thinking.
- Books need to be studied with authorial intent.
- Hermeneutics is the study of interpretation.
- The reason one needs to study the Bible is because it is a life-and-death, heaven-and-hell, situation.
- The best way to share the truth of the Bible with people preset against it is to share the Law before sharing the Gospel.

Exercises

- Write a list of your presuppositions, including your worldview and ultimate source of authority.

1.
2.
3.
4.
5.
6.
7.
8.
9.

- Write down your background, including upbringing, work experience, social economic status, and religious background.

1.
2.
3.
4.
5.
6.
7.
8.
9.
10.

- Consider your presuppositions as well as your background, and keep in mind how they will influence your study of the Bible. What are some ways that will do that?

1.
2.
3.
4.
5.
6.
7.

Three Reminders

1. Remember that your presuppositions are not bad. They just need to be checked at the door when you are studying a passage of scripture.
2. Remember as you are studying scripture that it is not about what it means to you but what it meant to the original audience.
3. If you come up with an interpretation that is contrary to two thousand years of church history, then you are wrong.

Chapter 2

Cut through the Ox Manure

Christ has spoken in the Bible, and He holds us responsible to understand, interpret, obey, and teach what he has said.

—John MacArthur[1]

Big Ideas

- Bad presuppositions about the Bible are really wrong.

- The question "How can we trust what the Bible says when there are so many translations?" is an ignorant question.

- The Bible being translated into different languages just means the Bible is very popular.

- The Bible was originally written in Greek, Hebrew, and Aramaic. No doctrine is affected by translating the Bible from the original text.

- Textual criticism has proven the trustworthiness of the Bible.

- When the Bible is compared to different English translations, there is no major change in meaning.

- People who use arguments like that are liars, deceived, or willfully ignorant.

Translation Table

KJV	NIV	ESV	NASB	NLT
If an ox gore a man or a woman, that they die: then the ox shall be surely stoned, and his flesh shall not be eaten; but the owner of the ox shall be quit. But if the ox were wont to push with his horn in time past, and it hath been testified to his owner, and he hath not kept him in, but that he hath killed a man or a woman; the ox shall be stoned, and	If a bull gores a man or woman to death, the bull is to be stoned to death, and its meat must not be eaten. But the owner of the bull will not be held responsible. If, however, the bull has had the habit of goring and the owner has been warned but has not kept it penned up and it kills a man or woman, the bull is to be stoned and its owner also is to be put	When an ox gores a man or a woman to death, the ox shall be stoned, and its flesh shall not be eaten, but the owner of the ox shall not be liable. But if the ox has been accustomed to gore in the past, and its owner has been warned but has not kept it in, and it kills a man or a woman, the ox shall be stoned, and its owner also shall be put to death. If a ransom is	Now if an ox gores a man or a woman to death, the ox shall certainly be stoned and its flesh shall not be eaten; but the owner of the ox shall go unpunished. If, however, an ox was previously in the habit of goring and its owner has been warned, yet he does not confine it and it kills a man or a woman, the ox shall be stoned and its	If an ox gores a man or woman to death, the ox must be stoned, and its flesh may not be eaten. In such a case, however, the owner will not be held liable. But suppose the ox had a reputation for goring, and the owner had been informed but failed to keep it under control. If the ox then kills someone, it must be stoned, and the owner must also be put to

death. [30] However, the dead person's relatives may accept payment to compensate for the loss of life. The owner of the ox may redeem his life by paying whatever is demanded. The same regulation applies if the ox gores a boy or a girl. But if the ox gores a slave, either male or female, the animal's owner must pay the slave's owner thirty silver coins, and the ox must be stoned.

owner also shall be put to death. If a ransom is demanded of him, then he shall give for the redemption of his life whatever is demanded of him. Whether it gores a son or a daughter, it shall be done to him according to the same rule. If the ox gores a male or female slave, the owner shall give his *or her* master thirty shekels of silver, and the ox shall be stoned.

imposed on him, then he shall give for the redemption of his life whatever is imposed on him. If it gores a man's son or daughter, he shall be dealt with according to this same rule. If the ox gores a slave, male or female, the owner shall give to their master thirty shekels of silver, and the ox shall be stoned.

to death. However, if payment is demanded, the owner may redeem his life by the payment of whatever is demanded. This law also applies if the bull gores a son or daughter. If the bull gores a male or female slave, the owner must pay thirty shekels of silver to the master of the slave, and the bull is to be stoned to death.

his owner also shall be put to death. If there be laid on him a sum of money, then he shall give for the ransom of his life whatsoever is laid upon him. Whether he have gored a son, or have gored a daughter, according to this judgment shall it be done unto him. If the ox shall push a manservant or a maidservant; he shall give unto their master thirty shekels of silver, and the ox shall be stoned.

Exercises

- Look at your list of presuppositions, and see what prejudices you might have against scripture.

1.

2.

3.

4.

5.

- Pray to God to help you overcome your prejudices that He would show you Himself in scripture. God will show Himself to those who seek Him.

- If you want further evidence on the reliability of scripture, I suggest reading *New Testament Reliability* by Todd Friel and Dr. James White, available at the Wretched Store at www.wretched.org.
- Compare the different translations, one to the others, to get a better understanding of the text. Just stay away from the New World Translation.

1.

2.

3.

4.

5.

6.

7.

8.

9.

10.

11.

12.

13.

Chapter 3

Study the Passage

The process of interpreting and grasping the
Bible is similar to embarking on a *journey*.
Reading the text thoroughly and carefully
lies at the beginning of the journey.

—J. Scott Duvall and J. Daniel Hays[1]

Big Ideas

- Since the Bible was written a long time ago, there are barriers to understanding the text.
- Some of the barriers are language, culture, time, covenant, etc.
- Understanding the author and audience is crucial to understanding the text.
- One needs to find out the complete thought of the passage to understand it.
- Surrounding context, book context, scriptural context, historical context, cultural context, and Gospel context need to be studied to understand the passage.
- God expects people to be responsible for their animals.

Exercises

- Determine the extent of the passage and why.

- Read the book of Exodus several times to understand the passage in its context and get a feel for the book. Read it at least four times. Some Bible teachers recommend at least thirty times to get a good grasp of the book.

- Find the theme and structure of the passage.

- Who is the author of Exodus?

- What is the date of Exodus?

- Who was the original audience?

- What covenant was Exodus written under?

- What is the theological theme of the passage?

- What is the surrounding context of Exodus 21:28–32?

- What is the book context?

Chapter 4

What Do We Do with It?

Measure the width of the river to the Cross. What are the differences between the biblical audience and us?

—Todd Friel[1]

Josiah Nichols

Big Ideas

- Differences between the covenants do not mean there are contradictions in the Bible.
- The Old Covenant had different promises, mediators, and rituals.
- The Old Covenant was stricter than the New Covenant in its rituals, ceremonies, and government.
- The sacrifices could not take away sins (Hebrews 9:7).
- The Old Testament was used as a means to show the Israelites their sin and their complete hopelessness to live up to the laws of God.
- The New Covenant is mediated through Jesus Christ, and salvation is through repentance and faith in His sacrifice on the cross.
- The original audience, covenant, and circumstances need to be taken into consideration before interpreting the passage for oneself.
- Three different ways of interpreting how to apply the Old Testament are only following the moral law, following all the Old Testament Laws except what the New Testament fulfills, and only following what the New Testament repeats.

Exercises

- Compare yourself with the original audience. Look at language, government, culture, time, covenant, and whatever differences you discovered in this chapter and the previous chapter.

- With what situations would the passage fit?

1.

2.

3.

4.

5.

6.

7.

8.

9.

- Would you ever be in those kinds of situations?

Josiah Nichols

- Look at a conservative commentary on Exodus and/ or a study Bible. I recommend the _MacArthur Study Bible._

Chapter 5

What Can I Learn?

Although this passage does not apply to us today, there are still things we can learn from this text.

—Todd Friel[1]

Big Ideas

- When one looks at the passage and understands what it meant to the original audience, then one can draw theological truths from the passage.
- Principles are general truths that can be applied to many different situations.
- Some principles that can be drawn from Exodus 21:28–32 are God values human life over animal life, God holds us responsible for our property, God is OK with the death penalty, God is for saving life, God hates wrongful profit, God cares about the lives of all classes of people, God hates neglect, and God understands situations are complicated.
- Compare the principles with other Old Testament scriptures to see if they are true.

Exercises

- Generalize the passage, and find some principles and implications of the passage.

- Look at what it meant to the original audience and compare it to you.

- Compare the different covenants.

- Look at these principles and compare the theology with *Biblical Doctrine: A Systematic Summary of Biblical Truth* by John MacArthur.

Chapter 6

What Does Jesus Change?

In that he saith, a new covenant, he hath made the first old. Now that which decayeth and waxeth old is ready to vanish away.

—Hebrews 8:13 (KJV)

Big Ideas

- The New Covenant changes the way the Old Covenant teachings are applied.
- Believers cannot do capital punishment unless they have been authorized by the government.
- Principles need to be timeless theological truths in order for Christians to apply them.
- God still values human life over animal life.
- God still holds us responsible for our property.
- God still is for saving life.
- God still hates wrongful profit.
- God still cares for all classes of people.
- God still hates neglect.
- God still understands situations are complicated.

Exercises

- Take these principles and the principles that you came up with, and ask what they look like in the light of the New Testament.

- Read the New Testament all the way through with
  your passage in mind.

Chapter 7

Kill the Ox

We teach that, whereas there may be several applications of any given passage of Scripture, there is but one true interpretation.

—John MacArthur[1]

Big Ideas

- While there is only one meaning of the text, there can be several applications the Christian can apply to it.
- Since principles are timeless theological truths, they can be applied multiple ways in different situations.
- While the above principle is true, there are some ways a principle can be applied.
- One needs to consider how a principle can be applied in one's personal life as well as in one's community, job, nation, and relationships.

Exercise

- Apply the principles you have discovered in different life situations.

Chapter 8

Come to Jesus

Secure sinners must bring the thundering of
Mount Sinai before we bring them to Mt.
Zion.

—George Whitefield[1]

Big Ideas

- If someone just interprets the Bible correctly, if they do not repent of their sin and trust in Jesus, they will go to hell.
- One can springboard from a passage to share the Gospel of Jesus Christ, even if the passage does not refer to the Gospel.
- A passage from the Law can be used to springboard to the moral Law, which shows the need for Jesus.
- This is not part of the interpretation process but a way to use what you have learned to share the Gospel.
- The Law reveals we are lying, thieving, blasphemous, and adulterous murderers at heart.
- We deserve to go to hell, a place of eternally conscious torment, for our sin.
- God is merciful and desires to save sinners.
- God sent His Son, Jesus, to live a sinless life, die on a cross to bear the penalty for our sin, and rise from the dead to give a newness of life.
- God demands that all men repent of their sin and trust in Jesus for their sin to be forgiven and have a new relationship with Him.

- When believers repent and trust in Jesus, they are sealed with the Holy Spirit and will have eternal life.
- God commands all Christians to share the Gospel with the lost.

Exercise

Go and share the Gospel.

Bibliography

Chapter 1

1. George Whitefield. "The Seed of the Woman and the Seed of the Serpent," *Selected Sermons of George Whitfield* (Christian Ethics Ethereal Library, July 16, 2009). Kindle Edition.

Chapter 2

1. John MacArthur. *The Truth War: Fighting for Truth in an Age of Uncertainty* (Nashville: Thomas Nelson. 2007), 156.

Chapter 3

1. J. Scott Duvall and J. Daniel Hays, *Grasping God's Word: A Hands-On Approach to Reading, Interpreting, and Applying the Bible.* 2nd ed. (Grand Rapids: Zondervan, 2001), 19.

Chapter 4

1. Todd Friel. *Herman Who? Read It Right, a Hermeneutics Primer* (Burning Bush Communications, 2001).

Chapter 5

1. Todd Friel. *Herman Who? Read It Right, a Hermeneutics Primer* (Burning Bush Communications, 2001).

Chapter 7

1. John MacArthur, *The MacArthur Study Bible* (Nashville: Thomas Nelson, 2006). 2003.

Chapter 8

1. George Whitefield. "The Seed of the Woman and the Seed of the Serpent," *Selected Sermons of George Whitfield* (Christian Ethics Ethereal Library, July 16, 2009). Kindle Edition.

Great Resources for Further Study

- *Herman Who? Read It Right, a Hermeneutics Primer* by Todd Friel at wretched.org
- Wretched Radio hosted by Todd Friel at wretched.org
- Apologetics Live with Andrew Rappaport, Justin Pierce, and Anthony Silvestro
- *Drive by Theology* by Todd Friel
- Answers in Genesis at answersingenesis.org
- Articles at Striving for Eternity at strivingforeternity.org
- *On the Origin of Kinds* by Anthony Silvestro at strivingforeternity.org
- *What Do They Believe?* and *What Do We Believe?* by Andrew Rappaport
- *The MacArthur Study Bible* at gty.org

- *Romans Roadblocks* by Josiah Nichols available at amazon.com
- *What Does It Mean to Me? A Pocketbook Guide to Biblical Interpretation* by Josiah Nichols available at strivingforeternity.org and tractplanet.com

Personal Notes

Personal Notes

Personal Notes

Personal Notes

Personal Notes

Printed in the United States
by Baker & Taylor Publisher Services